Nightflights
New and Selected Poems

Poetry by John Greening

Westerners (Hippopotamus Press, 1982)
Winter Journeys (Rivelin Press, 1984)
Boat People (Mir Poets Twelve, Words Press, 1988)
The Tutankhamun Variations (Bloodaxe Books, 1991)
Fotheringhay and Other Poems (Rockingham Press, 1995)
The Coastal Path (Headland, 1996)
The Bocase Stone (Dedalus Press, 1996)

John Greening

Nightflights
New and Selected
Poems

*May your flights of imagination
lead you somewhere extraordinary —
thanks for your contributions this week*

John Greening
Blinkin Ling
2005

Rockingham Press

Published in 1998
by
The Rockingham Press
11 Musley Lane,
Ware, Herts
SG12 7EN

British Library Cataloguing-in-Publication Data

A catalogue record for this book
is available from the British Library

ISBN 1 873468 61 X

Printed in Great Britain
by Biddles Limited, Guildford

Printed on Recycled Paper

For Katie and Rosie,
my prospective readers.

Acknowledgements

The poems are arranged chronologically according to the publication date of each book, which is in most cases also the order in which they were written: *Westerners* (Hippopotamus Press, 1982), *Winter Journeys* (Rivelin Press, 1984), *Boat People* (Mir Poets, Words Press, 1988), *The Tutankhamun Variations* (Bloodaxe Books, 1991), *Fotheringhay and Other Poems* (Rockingham Press, 1995), *The Coastal Path* (Headland, 1996), *The Bocase Stone* (Dedalus Press, 1996). Thanks to the editors concerned for their permission to reprint.

The complete "New English Edda" featured in Vol 76 Nos. 1/2 of *Poetry Review* (1986): it was written after *Boat People*, though published before that pamphlet came out. Some of the new poems first appeared in *Critical Survey, The Dark Horse, The Interpreter's House, Lines Review, Poetry Review, Poetry Wales, The Poet's Voice, The Review* (Canada), *Stand, The Swansea Review* and *The Times Literary Supplement*. The "Winter Journey" sequence, which first appeared from Rivelin Press, was reprinted in the later Bloodaxe collection.

Contents

from *WESTERNERS* (1982)

Notes to poems from *Westerners*   10
Westerners   11
Drive to a Temple   12
Ushabti   13
A Date from Nubia   16
Sweet Morning Tea   18
The Black Land   19
The Wife of Nakht-Min, a King's Son   21
Nefertiti in the North   23
Philae   25
The Crack   26

from *WINTER JOURNEYS* (1984)

Sonnets from 'The Winter Journey'   28

from *BOAT PEOPLE* (1988)

Sy Mui   32
Refugee at the Tatties   33
A Refugee Writes his Name   34
Hwa and History   35

THE NEW ENGLISH EDDA   37

from *THE TUTANKHAMUN VARIATIONS* (1991)

The Ash   46
Sweet Chestnut   47
Cromwell to his Wife, Elizabeth   48
King John Crosses the Wellstream   50
The Lists of Coventry   52

Howard Carter at Swaffham   53
The Treasures of Tutankhamun   54
White Cliffs   55

from *FOTHERINGHAY and other poems* (1995)

Nightflights   56
from Huntingdonshire Eclogues   57
Satellite   63
Seven Sea Interludes   64
Building the Boat   66
Katie in a Prospect of D.C.   67
Rosie in a Retrospect of D.C.   68
Geese   69

from *THE COASTAL PATH* (1996)

The Big House Ceremony   70
Ice-Hockey in Time of War   72
The Empty Quarter   73
Hoops   75
from Roads   76

from *THE BOCASE STONE* (1996)

The Bocase Stone   77
Horse Chestnut   78
Listening for Nightingales   79
John Gurney at Bedford Midland Station   80

NEW POEMS

Orpheus, Eurydice, Hermes   83
Rhineland Sonnets
    To Johannes Gutenberg   86
    The Praxis of Dr. Sandmann   86
    Schloss Rheinstein   87

Rhine Journey 87
Weingut 88
For Lotte Kramer 88
und Drang 89
Making it Clear 90
Heidelberg 91
Ballad of the B-17 92
Birch 96
Sycamore 97
The Twilight of the Birds
The Lodge, Sandy 98
Garden Début 98
Interlude 99
Gaudeamus Igitur 99
Heimdall 100
OM 100
Of Paradise 101
Dodo 101
Cage-bird 101
Tring 102
Night Calls 103
The Golden Treasury 104
Holst 105
Quartet for a Row of Terraced Cottages 106
Death in Aldeburgh 107
Hepworth 108
At Port Gaverne 109
The Source
The Source 111
Richard Burton 112
John Speke 113
Isabel Burton 114
Samuel Baker 115
Florence Baker 116
Snay bin Amir 117
The Temple of Horus 118

NOTES to poems from *WESTERNERS*

These poems were written while on two years' voluntary service in Aswan, Upper Egypt, 1979-81.

Westerners (page 11): The west was the home of the dead who were known by the ancient Egyptians as The Westerners.

Ushabti (page 13): Egyptian tombs often contain little 'shabti' figures with spells written on them to act as servants in the life beyond.

A Date from Nubia (page 16): Thousands lost their homes when the High Dam flooded Nubia. The Nubian people were transferred to desert estates far from the Nile on which their culture had depended.

The Black Land (page 19): The ancient name for Egypt, the blackness being the precious silt of the annual inundation. It is customary for pilgrims returning from Mecca to decorate their walls with scenes from the journey. A 'sayeedi' is an Upper Egyptian. Bilharzia and trachoma are diseases, horrifyingly common.

Nefertiti in the North (page 23): Akhenaten's consort appears to have fallen out with the heretic Pharaoh at some point. Smenkhare was their son-in-law, who became co-regent when the Aten cult was disintegrating. The description of Nefertiti ("the beautiful woman has come") is based on the most famous images of the Queen, particularly the Berlin bust.

Philae (page 25): Philae Temple – sacred to Isis – was taken apart stone by stone and reconstructed above Lake Nasser's water-level. Myths tell how Osiris' brother cut him into pieces, which Isis managed to fit back together – all except the penis.

The Crack (page 26): In Aswan's ancient granite quarries there lies an unfinished obelisk. Had a crack not appeared, it would have been the biggest ever made. Cleopatra's Needle, on the banks of the Thames, is from the same quarry.

Westerners

we ferried our past across here
our furniture   our favourite things
the familiar parts of our life

we reconstructed them to make
ourselves an opulent future
and barricade oblivion

you will recognise us among
these everlasting earth-treasures
in a gold mask   or in black granite

in the clean slot of a hieroglyphic
though you thought we were dead and strange
you will recognise us we are

still here   we are the westerners

Drive to a Temple

In the back seat
we are nearly all sweat.

Our Muslim driver
switches the steering to overdrive
and concentrates on smoking.

It's a tense route from the city:
the desert would like to gorge our car
and regurgitate a god

but the road's taut,
it holds us fast on our impulse

that the ancient sight
is a bulb we have to light
before the sun goes.

Now the last of our fingers
have melted into the plastic seatbacks

and our white Peugeot just holds
another stone-frayed curve

we hit a prayer

the window and the mirror
spin grey matter

dry mouthing   dried infinity

Ushabti

we are guests in a tomb
with that familiar mean muzzle

who will stretch himself and his bones
over any gilded chest   guard

with his cudgel tail
in his black coat
ears alert like bayonets

a culture
in unguents

the entrails of the Lords
Carnarvon, Cromer, Kitchener ...

we are guests
in a tomb

where there are ushabtis
for every day of the year

and the lady of the house
has given us one

fragile in faience
its name faint

a statuette
of the kind excavators kick
to get at the sealed bonanza

we are learning how to speak
to our ushabti
thus:

O ushabti

should I be requested
to do hard work
of the kind
that has to be done
down there

instead of it always being me
who sows the fields
fills the water-courses
and carries the sand from east to west

you do it
you do it for me

husband
killed
in 67

four times a week
forty pounds a month
three children
one room
the other side of Cairo
she pushes
on to the two-piastre bus

only the days
the lady of the house
is getting her hair done
horse-riding
or rehearsing *Iolanthe*

can she work
in time

today she can't keep up

she pushes
till she pushes

14

(crack
and wel-wel-eh!)

      'the antique marble ashtray
      they gave me
      when I went to Barcelona'
off
      'the inlaid table
      they chose for me
      in Dar'
on to
      'the hand-made carpet
      they presented me with
      before I came from Abadan'

ash
from umpteen
ambassadorial do's

      'irreplaceable –
      it's the sentimental –'

crack
and wel-wel-eh

horned
bi-focals
wind sideways

venomous
dentures flash

      'there are two crates of duty-free
      in the boot –
      bring them up for me!'

and the ushabti answers
here I am
here I am
I will do it

A Date from Nubia

More than whisky warms
the heart on a balmless

February night,
Shukri, creaking to the gate

in a thin gallabeya
and a gone-home pair

of my old socks
warms it with his jokes

and his devilish winks
as he smiles 'ideeni whisky!'

and we slap hands and laugh!
But he wouldn't touch the stuff,

he's a Nubian, the Koran
on his lap. In Ramadan

he won't swallow
his saliva, let alone

a scotch. When he prays
it's five times down on his knees

at dawn, at noon,
in the afternoon, when the sun's

just gone, and in the evening.
If a stranger should ring

and interrupt him, he'll welcome
you with tea and then resume

from scratch, but only after
insisting you accept the offer

of a date – saying, except
fresh like gold dropped

from the palm you could chew
to the breathing of the buffalo

water-wheels, he has no taste
for them himself; but a guest

like you, who's off
to Abu Simbel or to photograph

the High Dam, must eat
one dried date

as a commemorative act:
the last time dates were picked

in Nubia, Shukri had
teeth, and Nasser wasn't dead.

Sweet Morning Tea

The fan smiles
and shakes its head consolingly –

that fierce blue gaze
that withering yellow tongue –

this afternoon is inconsolable!

As evening
when the fan is sleeping
and she's allowed out veiled
I have found she's a cool companion

but as night
in star-dropped nakedness
then the questions wink:

Why did you ever leave your home
when everything
your everything
and everything you are is there?

Perhaps you couldn't appreciate
through all those domestic stirrings
all those teacup storms
the excellence of the white bone china.

Perhaps you will
when your cool companion
in her tomorrow dress
brings you her sweet morning tea

and the glass burns you
and the drink is black, without milk.

The Black Land

in variegated heaps
in a field
in the sun

dates ...

and other dried fruit
thresh dust
blacken
obeying a plough
urging primordial buffalo
to work the cogged wheel
another season

all
unalterable

except
forty million
are on the fly-strip

buzz
jostle

trachoma in empty eyes
bilharzia in full blood

the old red bus
bursting heat
and huge 'sayeedi' grins
will continue to shudder
through the shabby hens
and urchins

some black old women
get down

their home
their whole village
barely emerging
from sandstone

invisible
at more than donkey-speed

a tunnel-vault
a turreted wall
whitewash
with poster-colours
of a Boeing
lumbering off to Mecca

The Wife of Nakht-Min, a King's Son

(Cairo Museum)

His fat hands waggle, the policeman laughs,
and the loafing attendant licks the feather-duster handle.
All grease the glass with their noses, all pass the case
and take a snap. But some glance a second longer.

Her face, mutilated for reasons we don't know,
is still sufficiently fine to make us wonder
what else she hid behind the huge coiffure
fastened there like a cask of wine four thousand years.

Though the eyes and the lips have been destroyed
and a carved gold band is clamping the skull
so the plaited and tressed triumphal pylons
chain her in hair from head to chest,

she can still gaze and smile undamaged
through the small favours her sculptor bestowed:
a lotus-flower opening under claw-tight buds;
pomegranates tucked beneath a barren strip of gold;

how the sheaved and stately queen comes firm and small
into a ripe young girl where the corkscrew curls run out;
how the severed hand that should have reached towards
                                the king's son,
though severed, still clutches at some carved frippery;

and how an inspiration – the film of pleated
fine linen – ripples through indurated stone
to reveal the shapely abdomen and nubile curves
light, below the weight of a wifely crown.

my lover
I like to go to the lake with you
and wash there
allowing you to see me
wet
in my linen gown
of pure white

Nefertiti in the North

Not to be closer
to the roots
of this rose

in lands
where they say the Nile
no longer flows

but falls
like the sunlight

not to be watching
the bird-catchers
crouch
where the gardens end
outside my window

and that same figure
on my wall

not for the paintings
of his nets and his dog
driving from the papyrus thickets
a slim-necked water-fowl

not for these

and not to be quenched
by the sight
of the sand's disregard
for his sacred boundaries

never to scoff in triumph

'the-beautiful-woman-has-come'
has come

but since the King
is in the south
in the company
of his dear Smenkhare

I have come
to this castle in the north

Philae

When he went to pieces
she collected
the fragments and resurrected
(save a short
bit a crab had
gobbled) the god Osiris.

Greeks and Romans
worshipped her; but no man's
claws would ever court
her out of his coma.
No crisis

– river dammed
    or temple drowned –

would surge her thoughts
from the dry sound
love made.

                    Paralysis.
Bedridden. Blind
with wear. Yet behind
this confused water
clear sunk mind
observed the stasis
in her sanctuary
shattered, mystery
dismantled, the heart
removed from history

and Isis.

The Crack

The Pharaoh has arrived in Aswan today:
being cheered off the barge, being greeted
by officials from the quarry; on his way

through the streets, luxuriously seated
in a palanquin, to supervise the long-planned
raising up of his newly completed

obelisk. Across desert, up the grand
triumphal causeway carved for this occasion,
he's escorted to where the workmen stand,

their faces smooth, as if the abrasion
of a fear, of a persistent nightmare,
had ground them away. Without expression

they watch their foreman whisper in an ear
and the quarry official gasp, fall dumb
and helpless and leave the foreman to steer

the guest away. He knows the worst must come,
but he can patch time, pointing out the vast
unyielding rock-face, and outlining some

of the problems caused by having to work fast
and make crucial cuts too quickly, with risk
of ruin ... Leading the falcon eye past

the hollow of a previous obelisk
which only the rock's good temper had meant
it was finished and erected in weeks ...

But the Pharaoh has begun his ascent:
lifted over the rock these men wrestled
to overthrow; shaded from rays they spent

long months exposed to, some of them pressing
the wooden wedges in the hard-worked slots
and dampening them to swell; some dressing

the hacked-out shape for the final cuts;
and all, even through the pink rock-dust, pale
as alabaster now, aware of what's

made out to quarry employees who fail
to finish their allotted task before
the Pharaoh comes. Today it's a fairy-tale.

But that day it was as if the earth's core
had pumped a deep black vein of evil up
out through the granite slab, and the men saw

the crack, as if they were watching a heart stop.

Sonnets from 'The Winter Journey'

In 1911, shortly before the First World War, three members of Scott's polar expedition undertook a thirty-six-day journey through the dark of the Antarctic winter to collect specimens of the Emperor Penguin's egg. The Winter Journey *is based on their story. The full cycle of thirty-six sonnets which appears in* The Tutankhamun Variations *(Bloodaxe), was written in Arbroath, one sonnet a day for thirty-six days, as we advanced into an uncannily severe winter, 1981-82, and towards another war – this time in the South Atlantic.*

1

Tonight the sun turns. It's Christmas. It's Easter.
It's a summer seaside holiday – on ice! In the distance
the tide crack groaning. But in here, it's roast
pemmican and party games – 'a magnificent bust!'

Birdie's donned a funny hat. Bill has an egg
Cherry's opened for the riddle. Through thick specs
he reads it: *Why is the Emperor Penguin
like the Kaiser?* Outside, the ice cracks.

Because – and Titus pops his toy gun,
Evans does the Lancers, and once again our glasses
are filled for a Coronation toast. *Because the one –*
(Even Scott smiles, moonlight on a concealed crevasse)

*Because the one won't take his colonies off the ice,
and the other won't take his eyes off our* – Laughter! Laughter!

And the laughter dies.

4

The Barrier, and soft snow. We can hardly budge
the sledge-runners. Hard crystal. Could be the Golden
Mile for all the progress after we've hauled
the two loads back and forth along the Barrier edge.

Too much oil, too much equipment! Then you've pulled
off your fur glove to get a firm grasp. What you haven't
yet grasped is that it's minus forty-seven
where your fingers are. But when you come to hold

your supperdish ... Oh for that plain boiled
snow, or tea perhaps, and a Huntley and Palmer's
Emergency Biscuit! The three of us curled
around our cups, we almost think nothing can harm us,

that we will be able to survive that soul-
destroying howl, this cage, the megaton cold.

11

They swing, they sway, silk curtaining, they flash like swords
or searchlights, lemon, orange, green,
whirling in the east. We lay back our heads

and gazed. Exhausted. Incapable of words.
Wagner. Drury Lane. The kinema. An underground train's
electric flash. Incandescent flickering leads

opening through the dark. Distant power-lines
at minus fifty. Ice-angels dancing. Will-o-the-waste
luring us. The ghosts of the other dead explorers.

We gazed. We were transfixed. Except near-sighted
Cherry, whose lenses were so utterly iced
up he missed the show! *But wasn't it so boring*

stuck out there? Deprived of everything Society
can offer? The bright lights! Didn't you get depressed?

14

Antarctica House, its windows are whirls
of bleariness, its furniture is draped white,
the rooms one long chill draught of dark

closed doors. Occasionally, a sheet unfurls
a stony sheen, or the leads in the tracery light
with a stained aurora, only to sink back to the stark

domain of silverware, cut glass, and engraved
mirrors huge as mountain corries. All the clocks
have stopped, their rotating suns permanently down.

All the beds, though invitingly smoothed,
are cold, unoccupied. And each of the household nooks,
that flaw with a spider, a beetle, or a mouse ...

Even the servants have gone. Then who was it passed
us in the butler's pantry, that tail-coated ghost?

16

When Houdini challenges them to bind him head to foot,
fetter him, snap handcuffs on him under six stout locks,
then have him screwed into, riveted into a plate-glass box
filled with water, which is then itself closed in; or put

into a strait-jacket, wrapped in thick canvas with straps
of hide and steel buckles, and requests to be hung upside down
from a crane off the top floor of the highest block in town
so he can demonstrate again the ingenuity of his escapes ...

there seems to be little to distinguish us. We volunteered
to be thrown into this dark. Asked to be snow-stocked, frost-
manacled, strapped in harnesses, immobilised.

We chose to battle against the clock for dear life, just to be cheered
and called a hero. And we, like Houdini, boasted
we could escape even frozen in a solid block of ice.

'Steadfastly, surely,' said the *Express* correspondent,
its twenty thousand tons of nothing slid
'like some movement of Fate ... as a glacier glides
to the sea' ... Steel bauble, diversion for the affluent,

a jerry-built toy! From the White Star, Bruce Ismay
is standing proud and smiling in the dock.
Twenty-two knots, yes sir! he assures us. Nearer New York
to Thee. Blue Riband in his eyes, a smile.

We are still at Crozier, listening to the wind rivet
its Ross Sea Dreadnought, Unsinkable,
to be sent north next Spring, parade tiptoe

in front of millionaires and aristocrats who'll have it
photographed and still not picture the unthinkable,
the cold, the dark, the seven eighths below.

32

We are caricatures who box between the slits
in the spinning rim of a toy. We are spun
to re-enactment on this wheel, for the fun
of experiencing continual defeat. Among the exhibits

in the Crystal Palace, beneath the curving lights
with organ and wind-machine, in wax: Birdie,
Cherry and Bill. The tableau, 'Victorian Murderers'
is next to ours, 'Edwardian Suicides'.

There is no getting away, there's little hope
of ever getting out of this. It was a hazardous
undertaking. Not heroes, three foolish men.

We are small figures in a crystal globe
turned upside down and shaken to a blizzard
by a child, who laughs, and shakes it again.

Sy Mui

Sy Mui is embroidering

her eyes' point enters a wooden o
her breath swells a small stretch of cotton
to a silken bird of paradise
a silken tree of heaven
silk wings on a green silk moth

Sy Mui is embroidering

the shapes blow from her home
ripple her smile
make her fingers gently quiver

the silkworm weaves
with a slow and circular exactness
and the green moth comes to leaf

Refugee at the Tatties

(after Tu Fu)

My spade, my long spade
with your white wooden handle
I lived by you
dug yams enough for us all

but these days
we all have to bend
to lift
what we can't even eat

on this exposed hill
two weeks
without the clothes
or the shoes for it

returning in the end
richer by pounds
of these unpalatable tubers
and with a little extra rice money.

A Refugee Writes his Name

By imagining the Old Man of Hoy
I can distinguish him from the others:
he is the eldest of our beginners,
and certainly the tallest, the craggiest.

A fisherman, he chose to trawl far out
the deeper shelves, chase with the refugee shoals
from Indo-China to Hong Kong to learn
in Scotland his name's new shape. H-o-i,

he navigates the skerries of that sound.
H: Orion, the house, his new-sprung bed;
o: an absent face, or a ten p saved;
i: like a bazooka ...   Vietnamese

names are for brandishing, they hold you sharp
to a stranger's eye. If your son was born
on the high seas, you christen him High Seas,
no muffled Jimmies, anonymous Jeans.

Again it's H-o-i, look, H-o-i ...
the characters are nets, lures on a line
to our strange boat, but if he can grasp this
(he looks at me) he'll cut free, sail home to Hoi.

Hwa and History

Hwa Hwa
dumb as your da

they laugh
they call her names

'Retarded,'
the staff remark

at whatever point
you may locate her
on the syllabus
she'll still be in the doldrums

Vietnamese Hwa

Her history teacher
who's giving them a test
about the Vikings
next Thursday
is trying to explain how
more than a thousand years ago
Eirik the Red's son
Leif the Lucky
stumbled on America

but it's Hwa's pudgy hand –
'Please, Teacher, what *ago*?'

we laugh
we call her names

because ago
is the blitzfeuds
that wrenched whole families
up by the roots
thrashing them out of their world-tree
to be wave-people

it is the old pagan sap
beginning to rise
and beat out
Lindisfarne, Sutton Hoo

ago is runes on standing stones
dragonships in burial mounds

and not
(where history
stops for Hwa)

Vietnam
nine years ago
when the bombs
decided on her home

THE NEW ENGLISH EDDA

THOR has gone from the thunderclouds.

He plans a final wrestling match with that
sinuous constrictor of the earth, his only rival.

Disguised as the red beard you might have glimpsed
behind the windscreen of a huge West German truck,
he follows the autobahns and motorways
which he believes are the tracks of Midgardsormr.

In the cab, his short-handled hammer has been concealed
so he can seem to change gear with it.

His ring, wrapped around with animal fur, he spins
as if his manoeuvres relied on combustion of oil, not
consumption of mead.

His customary drinking horn trails behind,
undetectable as anything but a long freight container.

There is a noise of thunder
as Thor bounces along the A45 from Felixstowe.

Those who know
will recognise the theatricality of the effect,
the shivering of a vast emptiness.

At the lights, Christ crosses to him
and asks to see his tachograph,
then tells him to breathe into a little bag.

The Heavens change their composition.

Thor stares in silence out of a grey cell.

FREYR erect on a Dorset hillside

watches a gold boar stomp through a field of wheat
threshing each swath with its steel tusks and opulent bristles.

This magical boar, once his,
the property now of a sybarite whose ritual groans and
                                        effeminate clatter
are neither in honour of him nor of fertility,
spurts a musty shower of chaff,
depositing loose trails of excrement.

Freyr – the butt of every hotel-bar innuendo,
the blood in all the upward glances of embarrassment,
the membrane of our maturity's adolescent screen.

Also a well-known tourist spot to which grave students come,
and newly-weds, or older couples despairingly climbing
in their search for fruitfulness.

That rich seam where the Cerne Abbas Giant was exposed
is almost exhausted now.

Only the daughter of the landowner
as she rides out from a Victorian manor
on a white mare
her white arms gleaming
still fills the god with the old potency.

He would have abducted her in his magic ship, Skidbladnir,
the ship he used to carry in his pocket.

But he has no pocket.

He stands naked, with his one possession.

And, at the white hands of the landowner's son,
Skidbladnir descends to spray another field with deicide.

FREYJA descends to the common, to her Valkyries

who immediately recognise the swish of plumage
and the touch of white fur.

She passes, smiling, among their fires and makeshift tents,
within the cupel of her lips and in that apple-green stare
knowledge of the future.

What is the news of Ragnarok?

She removes her catskin gloves, removes her feather boa,
accepts a cushion, and looks at the stars.

They are still there.

The fires of the peace-camp crackle.
Their heat, their light, intensify as she speaks.

The World Tree, she tells them, is at this minute quivering.
The World Serpent, she tells them, is at this second free.

There is no sound but the kindling, no light but flames,
and a solitary police blue flash.

The attack, she says, will begin with the Wolf's eyes.

And then the convoy:

Naglfar, constructed from the nails of dead men
and manned by a crew of rigid zero faces, giants.

You must await, she says, the one loud blast on my chauffeur's
horn.

The women cheer.

But who is that hissing?

39

Silhouetted in the blue flash,
a policeman emptying a fire extinguisher
over the women's fires.

Freyja notes his name.

The women disperse to guard
the Orange Gate, the Blue Gate, the Violet Gate
of the Rainbow Bridge.

LOKI is the nail in front of your speeding De Lorean,
the volt that overloads the grid,
the laughter that starts a final breakdown.

He is the misprint in the Japanese instruction manual,
the perjury in a computer bank, the weatherman's error,
the lover on a crossed line,
the scramble-code between two presidential suites.

He is the weedkiller in the lemonade bottle.

He was Hitler's 'big lie'
and the beam in Robert Oppenheimer's eye.

He is a loose tile on a heatshield, a hairline crack in a wing,
a virus in a ventilation-shaft.

He was that thud in April 1912, the newsflash in November '63.

He is living at Windscale or Sellafield or Windscale.

He is called Schiaparelli, James MacPherson, Cyril Burt.

He is the flash-gun
at the moment of royal infidelity.

He was the spark
in the stacks of the Alexandria library.

Loki

about to make his come-back to the West End

as the star in *That Great Charmer*
as the villain of another Hollywood B.

BALDR floating into the White House.

There will have been an unofficial agreement
with the newspapers, radio stations and TV networks
not to reveal anything detrimental.

He is Baldr the Good
and feels himself unassailable.

He will appear, puffing a white smile,
and make a heart-warming joke at his own expense,
then pose with his wife, his dog, his teenage daughters,
ensuring that he is seen to enjoy a milkshake,
an early morning jog, or a laugh with his coloured neighbour.

Baldr honours all life.
Baldr believes in the sanctity of marriage.
Baldr wants peace.
Baldr attends a non-conformist chapel.
Baldr is strongly in favour of the death penalty.

He will be simple, sociable, firm, plain-spoken,
clean and elliptic.

Remarkably like you and me.

So when, at last, a tape of his hamartia
starts to wind about and prey on this robust image –
although a myopic sound technician will have admitted
                                        pressing the switch,
lawyers will have been hired to ransom his reputation,
and every newspaper, radio station and TV network will
                                        be pointing the blame
to that black neighbour of his –

with one touch
from the unreeling evergreen

Baldr bursts.

Our heroic saint-bubble.

FRIG has returned from her annual tour of the sacred places,
the churches of the sheela-ne-gig.

Now she is home, you may pass the gate
and follow the grassy track to look for her covered car.

This grove is a Grade One Site,
'untouched throughout recorded history'.

Here you may find examples of the rare black hairstreak
butterfly and the wild service tree.

But this is not of any significance to you,
for it is your privilege to have been chosen for a mission
of more than Special Scientific Interest.

Frig squats beneath a canopy.

Her eyes are a shark's eyes, her dugs like crouching toads.

She has spread her thighs to the trunk of an Ash
that in ancient times was split for children to be passed through,
a long-abandoned bees' nest, its honey hardened into fly-blow.

It is your privilege, having cleansed the canopy and the car,
to bathe her, to give her the five-fold kiss,
and, letting the bird's-nest orchid crush the small teasel,
fall back into an ecstasy of sludge, a gradual mud-suffocation:

death, the Great Rite,
beneath a goddess's rampaging buttocks.

ODIN treads the forgotten runways
seeking a tree, a bough sufficiently high to hang himself.

He has attempted it from the masts of our oak-ribbed men-o-war,
from poles bearing the standards of our foot and cavalry
                                                    regiments,
from every street-corner air-raid siren he has attempted it.

And has learned since, that a single twig
from the World Tree, Yggdrasil, where it emerges
out of the retreating sands and clay of Eastern England
will do the job, and more effectively.

He draws out a flex,
lowers one end to a source of wisdom,
connecting the other to his own throat –

his good eye the dark lens of a television camera,
his blindness a bright monitor of himself

– then, far below, with a twang,
and in a jargon nothing can deflect, Mimir's voice commands:

Let Gungnir fly!   Out pops the eye.

Odin hangs like a crimson wind-sock.
From the wound drips poets' mead.

HOENIR longs to speak.

He longs to tell us what Sibelius heard
at Järvenpää, or Bruckner when he knelt to his last finale.

He longs to speak
of what has been written and then forgotten,
of how all things begin and end in silence,
lost or destroyed.

Of Bach beginning to interweave B-flat,
A, C, B-natural
Hoenir longs to speak.

He longs to tell us about the future –

how some will survive the gods' extinction
and nest in golden eaves
and join with the vanished songbirds
to drink the morning dew

singing of nothing.

BRAGI runs a small poetry press.

He publishes the work of the lesser known and little read.
He edits a magazine called *Kvasir's Blood*.

But Bragi finds that people are no longer very interested
in poetry

or in seeing life through baleen-ribbed metaphors.

They have other fish to fry.

They have their cars, their videos, their hi-fi.
They feel no need for words wrought into significant patterns,
words that require more than a quick scan
to glean instructions or the outline of a plot,
taut words that quiver against your cavity wall
and sing of the Aesir and the Vanir and the winning of the mead.

And the poets themselves don't know what they should be
writing about.

Not war – they have never experienced war.
Not gods – they have lost their belief in gods.
Not love – love has been discredited.

The rotation of themes has reached its fallow season.

On to the worked-out prairies,
Bragi is throwing blood and bones and ash.

In every furrowed brow he will sow new images.

The Ash

i.m. Jack Redon

the Ash is for you

because of its charcoal buds
because it conceals white magic
because it can hold all winter
creation's keys

because it is tough

because as a spear, a hoop,
a chess-set, a picture-frame,
or a stage brace
it will keep its elasticity

because it can make its own face up

first appearing with ruddy mountain cheeks
then in pale chorus
weeping through Twickenham gardens

then the scarred and grizzled hero
of some grey Norse epic

collapsing
to a sudden curtain

because it is like a chameleon
an old Polonius

because it can smile
heal advertise
mesmerise
and tell tall stories

because it was once Yggdrasil
because it is
the last of the species in our end game
Jack, the Ash is for you

Sweet Chestnut

Maturity is to know the star-shakes
in your heart. It is to have turned aside

and, despite the upright and the smooth, gone on
turning. It is to be twisting free of

one's roots, ascending to its very lip
the twin helix. To have observed each year

some fresh disfiguring lump. To have felt
the next ring splitting under the renewed weight

of spring. It is to have seen the spears
lifted, then a spiked mace.

On slopes of ash to have faced the eruption
of your griefs. To have flowered. To propagate.

Cromwell to his Wife, Elizabeth

Here in God's water-meadow
where the sun dips
like a fox's tail
and rises
dripping rich light
to paint the willows, fens,
and meandering River Ouse,
are there not greens enough?

Here with our children,
here with my darling mother,
and your most devoted maid,
here with these good workers,
good stout oxen,
are there not smiles enough,
Elizabeth,

that you pollute
a room of plain white
with oils
of the world's monarchy?

What is it in these proud faces
that has so fascinated you
that you can sacrifice your good sense
to one crown after another?

Is it because you are not a bit proud
and not at all majestic,
that you feel you have to let
vain shadows of Elizabeth
dance and play
above our scrubbed bed-head?

Or have you heard the Fen
whispering
that I should tear down

one particular face
and replace
his picture with my own –
to hang between your Richard
and your Bolingbroke?

Perhaps it is that you would
like to become Elizabeth
the Second, Elizabeth?

Look at the common people.
Keep your ears muffed and watch them
as they survive in unalleviated flatness.

Now look in your own dear glass,
Elizabeth,
and not at these weak-chinned,
weak-eyed strong men.

King John Crosses the Wellstream

Dysentery was our only chance.
So long as he had to keep dismounting

for a squat, we'd not lose track of him,
although the Fens kept trying

to draw a mist between us as we were hauling
his baggage-train from King's Lynn

through Wisbech towards the Wellstream.
But then, at the Estuary, the air

became as clear as that cut topaz
Pope Innocent gave to him, and at once

we knew that his sickness had lifted
along with the autumnal murk.

He breathed, looked north, and
said not a word (not even: were

his treasures all secure, his crosses,
his cups, his pearl-studded knife?) and

cracking another raw egg, beckoned
us on into the landscape's open mouth.

We heard the quicksand smacking its lips,
and the tide-rip's slobber; but he

was away off on the scent of cider,
swallowing his eggs whole, like a skua-gull.

Of the one hundred and forty-three cups
of white silver we have now emptied

into the darkening Wash, of the gold plates,
and of the crowns that have sunk like flatfish,

had he observed but one, or seen us attack
the thick cords binding his precious collection

of baths, valuing only – among the emeralds
and sapphires of the advancing tide –

a few more seconds gained, and up to our waists
and feeling the rear axle lurch,

had he but noticed our desperate tableau,
these fingers clutching the setting

shafts of his last pageant-cart,
and felt not hunger, not parricidal anger ...

But King John is in Swineshead now, exultant
no doubt, and panting praises at his

deliverance from the gut-ache, enjoying
a ripe peach, the first of the new cider,

assuming that one of his servants will be on hand
to bring him the crown jewels to finger,

and his favourite bath, with kingly quantities
of healing water from the Wellstream.

The Lists of Coventry

Then, it was just a means of arbitration,
ordeal by mass entertainment: two knights,
like glittering exhibition cases, armed,

escutcheoned, and embroidered, their chased
lances quivering at the opposite ends
of a concourse, waiting for the first trumpet

to send painted Swan and Antelope charging
down on painted Mulberry Tree and Lion;
or a more urgent trumpet – like the voice

of a ten-year-old trying to make himself
heard above his advisers, above the mob
writhing around Wat Tyler's corpse – to cry out

'Let me be your leader!', and in a
kingfisher flash of crimson and green-blue
velvet, prevent the bloodshed. A lover

of spectacle, and the colourful arts
of peace, King Richard stands up to flourish
words in illuminated filigree

from a goat-hide scroll ... and we recollect
that Pathé shot of Chamberlain after Munich;
or a dark-suited, bespectacled John Nott

stumbling through the lists of British losses.

Howard Carter at Swaffham

We know him: it's
the Carter lad who
painted dear Lady
Amherst's lap-dog

and the Vicar's old
bull-terrier, quite
without schooling – son
of our gamekeeper's son.

And if his imagination
pierces a tiny hole
in these venerable walls
and holds a candle

through to a room full
of wonderful things
but utterly foreign to
a decorously mounted

hunting party with
its fine equipage,
its whips and sticks and
stuccoed wooden courtesy –

then what is that to us?
Tally-ho! and on towards
the twentieth century: let
the boy be content

with keeping trespassers
from our noble pile;
or immortalise our
ailing Golden Retrievers.

The Treasures of Tutankhamun

The British Museum, 1972

I am waiting, like all the others, waiting
to open the sacred seal and discover
my future; and as I wait, this exhibition
snakes me through steel barriers to my golden
eighteenth year where I catch, amid the darkness
that enfolds a teenage Pharaoh's history,

glimmerings of a more personal history,
as if it had lain beneath the sand waiting
for me to come and dig into its darkness
in search of the famous Mask but discover
only in each glass case my own face, golden.
It is my coming-of-age exhibition.

All aspects of me are in this exhibition:
the child's chair and board-game are a history
of my early youth; my teens were that golden
dagger. This trumpet, this cow-bed are waiting
for me to experiment, to discover
in their cross-meshed passages of darkness,

in sexual unity and divine darkness,
the Goddess Hathor's milk-white exhibition
of her transfiguring powers: discover
between her lyriform horns all history.
The Necklace of the Rising Sun is waiting
to embrace us, its clasp is cool and golden ...

Each morning my hopes shoot greener, but golden
futures only bloom after months in darkness,
during nights of counting the weeks of waiting,
and now at this jubilee exhibition
I am persuaded that time and history,
are relative. Come, UCCA! and discover

to me the sacred light, let us discover
the place where we are to spend our golden
prime and inscribe our names on history,
as one young man did, emerging from darkness
at eighteen to become this exhibition –
the very thing for which we are all waiting.

White Cliffs

Whistling round into Shakespeare Cliff, where poor
Mad Tom led his blind father to the verge
of devotion, my only daughter saw
from the carriage window the darkness surge
in upon her. I comfort her with talk
appropriate to her three months of light,
sweet nothings such as Lear perhaps once spoke
to his beloved fool, before the night
tunnelled his wits. Still she will not settle.
I would have tried to lull her with that long
blank verse speech of Edgar's if I thought beetle,
chough or crow talked peace. But she wants a song,
so: *There'll be bluebirds over ...* Searchlights sweep
above these black white cliffs, and she's asleep.

Nightflights

Then (the Mauls say) the only airport here
was Heston, where Mr Chamberlain took off
for Munich. They had heard the peaceful cough
of his pistons from their greenhouse, whose bleared
panes crack with Boeings now so I can't hear
their words about the war, but see the rough
remains of their shelter and the stone cover
to their well, and wish ... But my parents' fear
permits me only to dream of those unseen
dark places. Nightflights wink into the west
across our hawthorn hedge, towards a Heath
silence has stamped out like something obscene.
I go to bed, and with a tightening chest
lie there, wait, listen, and invent a myth.

from Huntingdonshire Eclogues

I

Here it begins, with the rains of December
that emboss our new north-facing panes and play tom-tom
on the polythene skin across our porch footings.

Like a breath of the primeval: savagely alone,
confronting the spray from Kinder Downfall, or
New Year's Eve paralytic among the Trafalgar Square

fountains ... Just negative ions, I suppose, making
the stone lions whimper in the subterranean passageways
of my past. *Past!* our broken guttering echoes.

The water table must have been steadily rising all today –
a thought as cold as quicksilver threading a glass capillary.
The earth mother has lowered her pendulous warm front,

to lean so close above the bed where her water babies lie
that we may be cut off by our own daughter's bed-time.
Darkness is rolling in and the builders have all gone home.

They built the house across the lane on the site of a pond,
our neighbour tells us, and laughs at the thought that one day
it will inseminate that city couple's barren double brick ...

Behind them, a single field of darkness stretches hedgelessly
towards the Great Ouse. Our 'common stream', as brown
as a common hare, hides in its form there. It has been known

to close the A45. No traffic down the lane tonight,
except a pig-farmer's tractor trundling autumn slurry
away to spread, great wheels scattering pearls of muck.

VIII

March, and already the winds prove it. The *Hunts Post* tells me
the mad March hare can be seen in the open field these days,
boxing or lying low; but I have yet to see one. Wind

is all I have seen, or the effects of wind: one larchlap panel
in our fence had loosened and soon the boundary-line was snaking
wildly in the clay; so today a man has come with a steel rule.

The wind unnerves me. I cannot settle to anything; instead
of putting coherent words on the page, I find my eye is drawn to
movement in the lane: green fairy wands, and winsome ragged skirts

of my neighbour's weeping willow; or my ear is hooked on the
squeaky
drag of insulated cable where it coils into my study and my Amstrad.
Then zephyrs from the window touch, like an Aeolian harp, that map

of the Stonely enclosures: each strip becomes a string that sounds
an aleatory life: *Mary Hemmings Lands, Jona.Cuthberts Lands,
Geo.Rusts Lands*; there *The Orchard*, here *Great Meadow*, and where

our garden ends, the inscription *Hare Close*. The thought of a hare
concealed in that post-war enlargement, in that blank exposure,
where two dozen families scraped an anonymous living, is as chilling

as today's wind. Hares were thought to be witches' moon-creatures,
symbols of increase and of long life; seek them in stone-age caves,
Egyptian tombs; they're as elusive as fire; the hieroglyphic hare says

Exist. It suits the hare that our hedges have gone, it leaves
his ballroom free: one sunrise you may glimpse two dozen waiting
in a solemn circle; or at sunset hear one cry out like a child.

XI

He set crocuses and daffodils along Old Ford Lane
for others' pleasure. That we had noticed and admired them
pleased him immensely. As public, as rough-hewn, and original

as that concrete heart he laid before his sleepy wife one
St.Valentine's morning, and which still hangs beside the elm
stumps, impervious to disease. There was nobody else

we knew who would throw back their window and call from
dinner – *Have a claret!* – or *carrot* as I once misheard,
imagining some avuncular party trick ... His generosity

was a magician's black box. One evening, we returned home
beneath a vast umbrella of fresh rhubarb: eaten, it set the date
for our daughter's birth! The day David Llewellin died

there had been unlooked-for perturbations in nature, the kind
bards exaggerate when a great man has fallen, the kind
Glendower boasted for his own nativity *(Signs have marked*

me extraordinary). When we tried, your last weekend,
to visit Spring Cottage, we found the skeletal footbridge
washed by a new ford; what had seemed a senescent trickle

become a lethal tide. By the time six days had carried
that week to its end, the waters had subsided, one willow
shattered, the rest of the lane swept grey. Now, today

as I push our daughter across your bridge, the Kym lies
peacefully retired; and in the uncut verges, crocuses
give way to daffodils, St.Valentine to Persephone.

XIII

This morning's fierce debate (Mrs Thatcher and the Police State)
has calmed to thatched cottages and a faint aroma of pig ...
Our friends, who have battered themselves all year on the tubes

and against the bars of suburban London, have come here to recover
beneath these oaks. I walk them to the Stately Home and back;
but when our neighbour's trap comes clop-clopping through the mist,

they double-glaze: a clip from a Dickens film on *Breakfast Time*.
Nor will they believe that our newsagent closes today. I explain
you cannot change things too suddenly: he had those same blinds

down when a stray bomb blew news of the war on to the cobbles.
People like their Sundays left; their pram-resistant pavement
kept as it was; along with those ghetto-blasting church-bells;

even the Co-op has to dress up in Gothic script ... No, they will
never need the riot shields in Kimbolton; Cenebald knew a safe seat
when he saw one! And what would anyone want to change? Except

those few who, in scattered yet-to-be-modernised cottages (usurped
horse-kings, forgotten drovers, pleachers of hawthorn, hollers
of clay), do without double-garages and swimming-pools ...
This year two

such originals died: their names I never heard ... The developers',
the builders' names, the names on the cherished number-plates –
these I can't help but know. The lanes swarm with prospective buyers

out for a spin – seeds from a tough fast-growing urban species ...
Though all that ever seems to germinate is Leylandii: quick-
hedging that looks like the artificial grass they drape at burials.

XIV

Widescreen, to *Gone with the Wind* themes, the Spaldwick road
slow-pans you towards forgotten footage ... You spot the odd barn;
a token hawthorn butt; and countless anonymous farm-tracks –

but the tracks are too straight; harder than they need be.
Each barn, as you make your approach, becomes a corrugated hut.
The road unreels its title sequence but your senses are enmeshed

by the foulness of brussels, silage, or is it that dead hare
you swerved to avoid? You do not expect to find living things out here.
No house for miles and, apart from the bird scarers, bird-noise

would be the only sound if you were to wind down the glass: peewits'
low-level, high-volume aerobatics; or the viffing of skylarks –
like two half-witted, crack-voiced veterans of the old hundred:

make a joyful noise unto the Lord of Air-space! And so it fell
that half a century ago Dwight Eisenhower sowed the bulldog's teeth.
But there was no Golden Fleece; only, somewhere over the rainbow,

the Rhine ablaze ... Now, occasionally, in the summer, a coachload
of balding shades will pause on its way to the Madingley graves to hear
that this is the village where Clark Gable's suits were tailored

and none will be told the uncanny tale that the village keeps and
does not advertise: the local man who was up and out early jogging
the broken runways: who saw, what he saw which is said to have been –

but secrets are what the Spaldwick road keeps best: the mist
encloses them more surely than the perimeter wire seals Molesworth's lips.
Unnumbered aircrew must have left from here. Some perhaps returned.

After we'd been last night to look for the ghosts of ridge
and furrow on the snow-trimmed fields at the end of the lane,
The Winter Walk at Noon was my bed-time reading.

This morning, the river that lay flat in the field's lap,
passive as Cowper's hare, has broken into a wild rush –
a rip hisses across the gravel track to Gimber's End.

My neighbour is out complaining about the lack of ditches:
It's the council. These bloody houses. I don't care –
they can put up as many as they want now! And stiffly,

futilely, sweeps the water from his gate. Strangers
are stopping to watch the pageant: the country's new regime.
Why did nobody predict that this sorceress would arise?

Range Rovers glide across the surface. Estate and Saloon
approach: bald heads in their glass islands pray.
Minis turn back to St.Neots, to the saint of all Minis.

Noon is bright with the spirit of river nymphs:
the smallest hill looks the pap of a goddess. Reasonable
William Cowper keeps dropping words into my head as if to

dam these pagan emotions. *God made the country!* – but
my neighbour, who is dour and flat-voiced, replies
It's more like a town, these days ... The Independent arrives,

and on the front page is a Huntingdonshire tragedy: a mother
dives to snatch her toddler from the floods, and drowns. The father
tries to rescue her; he also drowns. Only the child crawls out.

Satellite

A dish points outwards from our outside wall
to what we cannot see: stars that know all
more clearly than these nightly Movie Greats
the fate of earthen empires. The new estates
that blinker us from crystal ballroom spaces,
haul us on in their fibre-optic traces,
plough constellations; with a flash of shares
u-turning, leave the Great and Little Bears
extinct, and gilt-edged bars of progress furrowed
down the land's face. All that we have is borrowed:
museums full of stuffed trophies slowly
decaying. Territories that tick. Holy
marbles seeming to breathe. Even these words I
mix to purity, and this island time
we live on, living off serials, then soap,
and lastly just news – that shooting green hope
our parents plotted as the world turned red,
not with sunset, nor shame, but foreign dead.
We wait, hungry, now we have cleaned the Great
from Britain, scraped it out, shrunk it, wait
for a force beyond this uttermost storey
of our high rise, a column whose glory
will be to have relieved us of our fame,
of all that mafficking, cheering of a name
picked blind from a skull and nailed to the sky.
The dish receives its message from on high
in beams that swaddle the earth; in curves
of parabolic reckoning. Then serves
us word made flesh: chained bare Salome sprawled
before us; while Civilisation's bald
chronicler slots between those repeats of Wars
for King and Country networked in the stars.

Seven Sea Interludes

I

Childhood is soft chalk: it allows the sea
to erode, almost to break through; were we
forever children, there would be no Midlands,
only sea air, a mirror-line of headlands.

II

Adolescence arrived like a storm beach
overnight, with bodies, much sea-wrack, and each
shingled face turning guiltily from salt
ejaculations to identify a fault.

III

Student days hang like a pantomime horseshoe:
that bay on whose shores we held our barbecue-
debate-cum-dance, loving the tides' motion;
aware, of course, from lectures, of the pollution.

IV

As young couples we kiss to the cliff's edge,
lie down with razorbills on a narrow ledge,
laugh at the lifeguard, laugh at the fishing folk
in their corky craft, the sea is a huge joke.

V

Executive schedules seldom cover
the seaside; only if there's a lover
or a business conference. One buys a yacht.
One moors it in Poole Harbour. The strakes rot.

VI

Parenthood is a final glimpse of the gold
you found on the beach as a one-year-old.
Return to the Landslip: the past gives way
and you are your children, have feet of clay.

VII

A Saga Holiday, perhaps. Promenades
before supper, an evening playing cards.
Images in a land-locked single room
of crossing the bar, stacks, arches; the blown spume.

Building the Boat

From holt and weald they drag
extinct pines to be our keel,
while someone chips a flint.

From the New Forest they roll
oaks to be carved to inflected
Norman ribs, while someone

is melting copper with tin.
The Greeks give us olive pegs.
The Roman inspectorate moves in

to mark our water-line. And all
is caulked with the bees-wax
from a dissolved distant priory.

On the prow is a plaque of laurel
with our dates and a painted eye
in green acrylic. Safely below,

and rigged in Egyptian white linen,
a Californian Big Tree someone
has forged a way of holding in irons.

But our oars are of Norse ash: heave now
towards the Black Sea whose huge waves
rear, long over and not yet.

Katie in a Prospect of D.C.

Outside the Oval Office
my daughter started
to sing Humpty Dumpty.

Then, at a rising black wall
that dropped to a V,
she stopped singing and cried

for a flag of stars
to wave past the dark
windows of the Space Museum.

On Capitol Hill, she
chattered towards a life-
size image of Jesus,

was silent before the statue
of the Father of Television,
heard the floor whisper.

But approaching Watergate,
she pressed her investigative nose
to the glass, and broke in

on our conversations again
and again to report
what all the king's men couldn't.

Rosie in a Retrospect of D.C.

This little toon
that giggles from the depths
of her sleep, flicking
muscles in dream joy

was less than a cel
until we came
to Washington in a hot
June three years ago

to catch up with the Air
and Space and touch
moon-rock and stand
beneath that battered

myth of Apollo,
visiting all monuments
to the word shot –
and it was hot

where she was conceived,
while the pumpkins
flowered in the dry yard
and the cicadas

wound their reels in
from the night, and we
were hooked on the
Little Mermaid video.

Geese

The in-formation
technology
of geese

can hear on its
high white
cirrus fibres

when the cold
is coming. Long
distance calls

awaken me each
morning. I lift
my head and let

the programmed
weatherline
croak on, watching

slack coils
of wire
stretch until

the message is
communicated,
then nestle

back to snore
snugly like
a warm receiver.

The Big House Ceremony

for Lee and Judy Harris

We have come to the Big House.

Only 100% natural materials were used in its making.
Spruce and sugar maple and fir.
And for the third floor something dark red and aromatic.
The windows are blinded and veiled in an invisible mesh
for our defence. The TV
is a totem pole
of a cable's length
that hypnotises the house.

Rockers await on the porch.
Dishes repeat and repeat their rain-dance.
Ice advances in its box.

And on our first night
The Big House Ceremony took place:

between these four walls which are the four grandparents
of a year which as yet blows in all directions –

under this roof which is a sky beyond the fireflies,
drug-zones, Interstates, and Late-night expending –

on to this floor which is the earth we crossed in a palm
that scalped the Old and blessed the New World's fontanelle –

came the one hundred guests to welcome us
(our beady monosyllabic reserve)

with fowl, fish, fruit and cakes of maize:

to welcome our pale faces
and laugh out deep from multi-cultural roots
names for us to harvest.

Beaming in rainbow shorts and mirrored shades:
But once you get acclimated ...

Embracing our embarrassment like Whitman
or that woman who wanted pizza
with everything on it!

Measuring distances in hours
ingredients in scoops
and sensibility in cents.

Not one of them smoking.

But hoping we have a peaceful stay.

And then to dance
around the golden
oval dance-floor
of their uniqueness

out-talking the cry from the Beautiful White Path

geese commuting from reservoir to reservoir.

Ice-Hockey in Time of War

A Midwinter Night's Game

Padded to look like men,
faceless, behind iron grilles,
and wielding sticks huge
as tactical battle equipment,
these dumb mechanicals swerve
across the ice and collide
with cheers from parents, packed
in front of hazy screens.

Every now and then a siren
goes off and the young
leave the arena like body-bags
while reinforcements are lured
on to the ice by a puck
that will reduce them all to asses.

December 1990

The Empty Quarter

on themes from 'Arabian Sands' by Wilfred Thesiger

Lionhead, foxpelt, oryx horns,
my old service rifles in their rack,
these tablets, this scotch, and a map

of the *Rub el Khali* ('What is he
talking about? What does he want?'):
the Sands, the Empty Quarter ...

Is it enough to remain an Englishman,
no longer The Christian? Or enough
to slouch, replete, and alone,

after a pork lunch, windows
Chubb-bolted against intruders,
their watch-towers, telephones?

Bismillah el Rahman el Rahim ...
Something calls from beyond this flap –
a wolf? The one that killed

two children at their water-hole?
Or my dawn summons – the profane
brass bell of a coffee-mortar?

Like a lighthouse I tower here, but –
El Nasrani! El Nasrani! – am conspicuously
inferior. These are Muslim, these are Bedu,

the 'English' is an unknown tribe,
or known as the Infidel. My excuses
parch: their Sands drink, drink.

Brick wastes of England. Dunes
that have gutters and aerials. Horizon
strapped to the wrist, our distances

are dates and coloured tubes,
Alum Bay egg-timers,
budgerigar and hamster cages ...

'Guide us on the straight path',
our minds are sand, stuffed
against the sun, against moon-raids,

not equipped for the shifting, sinking
one path, which is only camel-dung
(could be camel-dung, could be raiders ...)

I am alert. ('Better cold and wet
than to wake with a dagger in your ribs')
But what am I hunting? An extinct,

not mythological creature – and one
that could survive without this shell,
but only in deserts at the mind's end.

(1983)

74

Hoops

On Ash Wednesday
out come the hoops

to bowl open-
mouthed and breathless

through the rich dust
all morning, down

the long straight fen
causeway, wooden

and iron hopes
that the wind wants

to carry to
immaculate

conceptions in
Rome, to the end

of the Ermine
Way and Cardyke,

without one stick
having had to

strike, crying: we
are nought and praise

that we are in
fens of minus.

from Roads

1

Convenient, no doubt: a short-cut across
the site of Naseby Field, making at last
the M1 accessible. The past is past:
a haywain rutted deep; a dead shire-horse
blocking the way; the choice between your purse
or your life. So, never mind the open-cast
incision in our gut, or that the fast
lane overtakes these grey crawlers who cross
at night on ineradicable routes –
controlled explosions – rusted spiky mines –
or that these moon-shapes drop out of the air
to mate with kindred eyes of one who hoots
welcome, then obliterates the white lines.
Never mind, so long as we're getting there.

4

The first time we have let her on the road.
Her independence paid for with our fear,
as one small gold-and-silver frame goes veering
on to the verge to let a serpent-load
of scaly greens, a slurry-guzzling toad,
baleful giant, or dragon in red gear
that licks our hedges, pass. She's learnt to steer,
thank God, and signal too, the way I showed
last time we rode out. Nothing pleased her more
than my pronouncing her road-worthy, grown up
to join the brotherhood of spokeless wheels.
It's hard now to remember how it feels,
that first free-plunging run down from the top,
here on the far side of all she's waiting for.

The Bocase Stone

'That's the only happy thing you'll see today!'

this old guy muttered, easing himself out from
his ancient muddy Ford, the collie pup

bounding up to us, then furiously
away across imaginary borders.

A late October spell of sun, walking
Northamptonshire footpaths, one of them by

hawthorn and a leaning stone, its legend
IN THIS PLAES GREW BOCASE TREE there faintly

echoing hallowed stones and hollow creeds.

We follow a circular route, through mud
and mellowing beech-trees, with much to be

happy about, the unmerry stranger's
godspeed – a rhyme, a charm, a spell? – that shot

and missed as we were entering the wood,
long in the past, like the myth of Robin

hiding a bowcase in his day, fleeing
where we flick aimlessly, down the Green Lane.

Horse Chestnut

Grandfathers who have spiky outsides
can be fun inside: a gallows humour,
hanging their youth out to be hit

by kids who have not had to bake
or save, but possess proud fivers
on shoelaces they have grown out of.

Yet the young do not recognise the tree
in winter. Only now there is a hoard
to be scavenged from the park.

They do not think of it as an alien
or worry about it being too near
the house. They have their collection

of gleaming gladiators in a bowl,
and have no doubt that they will shine
right through and on beyond Christmas.

Listening for Nightingales

All the birds of the dusk
sound beautiful. Is there one
that sounds true, that empties

a dark jug drunkenly
as Grafham Water raises its
H_2O? Ah, Keats

I envy you your certainty.
I too would fly by nightingale
if I could be sure that that

that's like a spring stuttering
out of a broken pipe were the pure
original song, and not

a drug on the market. Such black
burdens the wings of my enchantment,
it plunges off the green grid

and there is nothing. That magic
flew with your age,
and leaves me in the dark with mine.

John Gurney at Bedford Midland Station

Bedford Midland. A stooping Horus hawk
above the mind's abandoned aerodrome
checks at the barrier. *John?* Our shock
dumb-synchronised. *John!* I in monochrome,
pain-striped for a funeral; you travelling
light to grandparenthood. And suddenly, in
one surprise roll, we are unravelling
a rainbow, enter an inverted spin
through ether, phlogiston, prana, to where
Egypt opens its lotus chute. Aerial
displays that – like the station signs we tear
past blindly – soon prove immaterial,
as King's Cross/St.Pancras brakes all dreams
but yours: you sit there, gliding to the Thames.

NEW POEMS

In the end the man turned from the music.
He studied numbers.
He forged a key to open the golden door of the sun.

George Mackay Brown, *The Journey*

Orpheus, Eurydice, Hermes

*translated from the German
of Rainer Maria Rilke*

That was the souls' astonishing deep pit.
They ran like silent veins of silver ore
across its dark. Blood gushed from under roots
and on out to humanity, with a look
as hard as porphyry there in the dark.
Nothing else was red.

But there were cliffs here,
and hazy forests, bridges over nothingness
and that enormous grey blind pond that hung
above its distant depths, a rainy sky
above a landscape. And between meadows
long-suffering, mild, materialised
the one path's pale stripe like a length of washed
white linen laid out.

On this one path they came.

In front, the lean man in his azure cloak
who looked ahead unspeaking and restless.
His stride devoured the path in hungry chunks,
not chewing them; his hands, leaden, clenched,
hung down out of the falling folds, oblivious
to the lyre striking deep into his left arm
like briar tendrils through an olive tree.
His senses seemed to have been split in two
so that his gaze ran on just like a dog,
turned round, returned, and ran ahead again
and stood waiting at the next blind bend –
while hearing lagged behind like an aroma.
Sometimes it seemed to him his ear did catch
the movement of those other two who should
be following throughout this whole long climb.

But then it cleared into the echo of
his own steps and his own cloak's after-gust.
He told himself they must be coming, though:
said it out loud, and heard it die away.
They must be coming, only
they move, those two, with a dreadful calm.
If he could turn just once (if such a glance
were not wrecking this plot so nearly perfect)
he'd see them, surely, the unruffled pair
behind him, in silence, walking.

                    The god
of travel and of distant messages,
a hood pulled down above his brilliant eyes,
a rod held out before him, and his feet
beating rhythmic wings about the ankles,
and there, devoted to his left hand – she

who was so loved that from a single lyre
more lamentation came than from lamenting
women, that a world of lamentation
emerged in which all nature rose again:
glen, forest, footpath, village, field, stream, wildlife,
and that around this Lamentation World,
just as around our earth, a sun, a heaven –
stilled and star-filled – was revolving,
a Lamentation Heaven, its stars defaced ...
she was so loved.

But moved now with that god in hand, her step
restricted by the lengthy winding-sheet,
uncertain, meek, and free of restlessness.
She was sunk in herself like one expectant
and did not think about the man who ran
ahead, nor of the path that climbed to life.
She was sunk in herself, and being dead
filled her like being full.

As full as is a fruit with dusk and sweetness
was she now filled with her own gravid death,
which felt so new she could not grasp anything.

She had entered upon a new virginity
and was unreachable, her sex closed up
like some young flower at evening, and her hands
so unaccustomed to the married life
that even those unendingly so tender
guiding finger touches of the god
pained her like gross familiarity.

She had long ceased to be that blonde-haired girl
who used to echo through the poet's song,
to be the wide bed's fragrance and oasis,
to be that man's belongings, long ceased.

She had already been let down like hair,
been made an offering like fallen rain,
been handed round like an endless abundance.

She had already roots.

And when of a sudden
the god restrained her and in a pained voice
let out the words: *He has turned round* – she could not
take them in, and murmured simply: *Who?*

But far above, dark at the bright way out,
there stood a figure, one whose features were
unrecognisable. He stood and stared
as on the stripe of footpath through a meadow
the god of messages with one sad glance
turned to follow that faint shadow, already
returning down along the track, her step
restricted by the lengthy winding-sheet,
uncertain, meek, and free of restlessness.

Rhineland Sonnets

1. *To Johannes Gutenberg*

You taught us how the world could be contained
between stiff boards, reduced to type, to a row
of lead: preserved, passed on by mirror-code
to any future, even this, where multi-laned
our information runs its rings, hare-brained,
and wails and mocks the passing of the slow
cold dawn of print on page. Books will still grow
as grapes are red. But look – this untrained
circuitry is cocooning us: no need
for labour here, the hourly vintage plays
direct from every lap, its icons bubble
a character from light with lightning speed
and disregard for all you hauled, screwed, pressed
out of the dark – yes, and thought immovable.

2. *The Praxis of Dr. Sandmann*

A spa. A casino. A psychiatrist
talks us across the bridge and then drives on
listening – where Brahms lived and Wagner composed
Die Meistersinger (the waters' prize-song
trilling its expense account), Dostoyevsky
was inspired to write *The Gambler*, and Goethe
dreamt of lemons, demons ... But we come to scry
the shape of my old German soul-mate's future:
the suite where he fights battles in the dark
with ghosts no other art can hope to touch
nor any sacred spring, nor sacred Mark
drive out. A croupier, he clears the couch
of dreams he sees flung down to him like bombs
unexploded under plush, peaceful homes.

3.   Schloss Rheinstein

The inner workings of the mind are here
laid bare. Melodrama scales each high tower
up spiral stairs to walkways where plots cower
across the air. It is the Castle Fear
unwinds its gothic opera past roe-deer
whose skulls are nailed on wormy painted shields,
past suits of iron, fossilised, yet filled
with thirty years' war. Schloss Rheinstein's beer
is always out of reach: on a dream terrace
glimpsed beyond a grille, through an arrow slit,
behind chains, up dungeon steps ... We hear a rumour
the Hare Krishna sect had wrecked this palace
till a *Volksoper* hero rescued it,
whose voice admits you now to the dark tower.

4.   Rhine Journey

The middle stretch is difficult, but I
have kept returning to that long ripe curve
and found it navigable, buoy-marked, safe
for any scribbling Siegfried to get by –
to blow his horn and set out heroically
each day. The middle-aged poet's groove
has dated, while Hildegard, rejuvenated,
sings hologram duets with Lorelei.
The vineyards on the terraces are locked
like monkish books, bound in their cells, loaded
with chants and *Minnelieder* and boredom.
The middle stretch has two sides: one of them –
unless you are a heroine encoded
in a fashionable ring of fire – neglect.

5. *Weingut*

These roots have reached four metres down to drink
through more than twenty harvests since I came
and drank myself at Sandmann's vineyard, the same
sight that blinks towards the Rhine valley's brink
on vine upon vine into that running ink
of thunder botching the high power lines.
Here, poetaster meets taster of wines
and each has air to clear – a grumble, a wink
between cloud and earth. Where the native soil
embarrasses with riches, a poem's breath
might raise a blush; but old dreams ripen
and must come to the press. In spite of hail,
however sour the grapes, or hard the earth.
The summers grow hotter, but roots deepen.

6. *For Lotte Kramer*

Mainz gushes, amazed at its own existence.
Its fountains swell a blessing in square havens
over bishop or drunk and, near St Stephan's,
a statue of three *Mädchen* huddled under
umbrellas. Today, there is threat of thunder
far off. Round these grey children all that's falling
is clean piped water. And a mother calling
she's found at last that special fountain lost since
we came here with one daughter. Now we've two.
And three endure a christening that still pours
after nine playful years. Only emotion
ran free when you left, many lives ago,
a city of dark looks and lightning jaws
from which there was no shelter but the ocean.

7. *und Drang*

On Wednesday comes the storm. The barbecue
will have to take to the cellar, and we
put on our guest masks. Outside, pleasantries
of Serbian spruce smashed flat. Lift the floor –
nobody hides here but a student of law
who wasn't invited to join the party
and who'll complain about the noise as we
make for shelter. It's as if this clear brew
of plum liqueur from the Balkans, home-made
and brought out by Croatians who now work
as *Gastarbeiter*, conjured from the air
the 1940s and the British raid
on Mainz, such a shattering attack
the cellar still cries its curse on *Engländer*.

Making it Clear

In Pitlochry, we said they were in danger
of breaking the china figurines,
so stop it. But on top of Craigower,
childhood tumbled in the hung-
over dregs of spilt heather
while an elder on the new seat,
sharp through Killiecrankie and Glencoe's
late April haze,
calibrated war: his job,
to locate the graves of bomber-crews
in Germany – 'bright green,
ye know there's something buried,
unless it's fish-guts,' he laughed.
Lochinver, where he lived until his wife's
heart gave out, there was this
greenness ... I mention the Clearances
and 'Aye, for some it's still
a raw wound, but more
made money fro' the burnings
and it couldna be helped – Culloden
had broken the clans.' Then,
the old historian pausing
before the young soldier's leap –
he wants to just make this clear:
'Dresden – Dresden was wrong,
that's all ye hear fro' the box
over and over, night in
night out, droning. Listen –
they were asking for their portion of stones,
they were Nazis to a bairn!'

In the silence
we fix on Pitlochry, its homes

cleared by distance to a grid
where none of the Good Friday
gathering of world clans,
no march, no reel, no air
raised by a tiny hand
that's touched a figure on a box,
can move us.
                'Shame,' he said,
'ye canna see so far today.'

Unbolting fingers, we let
our names drop, then swing
the children around, to run
for home, down a carpet
of needles, dead and soft.

Heidelberg

Climbing to the *Philosophenweg* in Heidelberg
with my parents, when my father was scarcely more
than fifty, he began to falter and to hug

my mother for support – as if this middling climb
were just too much, as if through fretwork he saw
all that he would in no time

be unable to do, how victory had run out,
how the things he'd promised war he would make
of peace were never going to come about,

the Neckar romantic below us, the bridge,
the castle, and at last the *Philosophenweg*,
a long and level walk, like retirement, like old age.

Ballad of the B-17

Gross ist der Männer Trug und List
                                        Eichendorff

The gunner lay beneath his girl
    and gazed beyond her eyes.
He saw the constellations wink
    clear warning from the skies.

Tomorrow you will fly, they said,
    your twenty-fifth and last.
Back home then, and back down to earth:
    this passion will have passed.

But he swore he'd never leave her,
    he swore eternal love
by everything that's holy – save
    that emptiness above.

He woke to ice and powdered egg,
    he woke to mud and spam.
His captain said: 'Your caffeine pill.
    We brief at 4 a.m. ...

'Your target will be Schweinfurt, men,
    Herr Hitler's steel plant calls.
A daylight raid –' The gunner said:
    We'll get him by the balls.

'And now I'll let the padré speak ...'
    The gunner smells the dust
and smiles: *that pin-up on our nose*
    is where I place my trust.
And kiss all four good engines –
    it's ball-bearings or bust!

It's farewell nights in Bedford
and be seeing you in clover,
it's *auf wiedersehen* Kimbolton Church
and spot the cliffs of Dover.

Leather, sheepskin, chute, Mae West,
have left the spirit bare
on a climb to 30,000 feet
through the frozen neutral air.

There's silence over the intercom,
the radio's one roar,
and ten young men alone in the sky
beside 3,000 more.

There's clear blue on the Belgian coast
but blackness deep inland.
The storm in these bolted bomb-bays
is Thor's own war-time brand.

It throbs its operatic props
behind a scrim of steel.
A small boy stares up through the clouds
to watch the news unreel:

then turns back to reality
and crouches in the dirt
to win that *Kugellager* from
his brother brownshirt.

The gunner's turret twists and streams
as fire erupts below,
cathedrals raise a stubborn neck
to the bombers' lava flow.

But on beyond where Rhine meets Main,
they hug their thunderbolts,
the gunner in his dream-ball dancing
last night's fairy waltz ...

The mild and bitter, jokes and lies,
    the tricks he used to win her,
as if he'd never had a wife
    in German Pennsylvania.

The gunner's mask is itching – round him
    swabs of flak begin:
If only I'd had time to shave ...
    The flak just nicks his chin.

And now the puffs come close enough
    to pebble the plexiglass.
A portside flash, no crash, but there
    a face and limbs fly past.

But where has the formation gone?
    And what is that shadow doing
slanting below their line of flight?
    That voice – 'Hell, guys! We're goin'!'

The bombs drop down. The smoke comes up.
    But somewhere inbetween
the gunner notices just too late
    one lost B-17.

The Messerschmidts are on your tail.
    Their tracers dart and dare –
the debris of great fortresses
    is falling from the air.

O you've lost your two waist gunners,
    the cockpit is blood and bone,
your ailerons are all shot up,
    gunner, you're on your own.

The bearings'll not get through now,
    the great iron wheel won't turn –
but you are caught in a blazing fort
    and the engines watch you burn.

A telegram ticks through the gunner's nerves
and worms out of his head.
It says *I regret to inform you*
and it smells of his unmade bed.

She will not be taking him back with a kiss
and a Pennsylvania smile.
He will not be sitting to reminisce
with a Pennsylvania child.

Below him the rock of Lorelei
reaches to break his dive.
The gunner remembers his Mae West and chute,
for many escape alive,
for many returned to Kimbolton
to fly their twenty-five.

The gunner lay on the Lorelei
face down in the mould:
her song blocked out the sun – *Kommst nimmer
mehr aus diesem Wald.*

Birch

Canoe or witch's
broom at the bottom

of the garden: escape
from the day of fire

or the day the scalp-
chilling ice-caps

grind their war-path
and our only comfort

against the red clay
in which we bury

frozen hoards
of gold and silver

is gold and silver
of the forest malls

where we will live on
postcards, bootsoles,

pennybuns and
bark-bread, bark-bread

Sycamore

Throughout late summer,
tipsy wasps had sipped
honeydew that our
sycamore let drip
on to moulded slabs.

We had to summon
a Red Cross Knight, clad
in white noise, to quest
with his chain-saw for
the sweet heartwood Grail.

Air will not play her
pentatonic scales
now, nor pink buds green
and fall into a
hollywood pastiche.

But teach violin:
between her shoulder
and her chin, its fine
striped body, buzzing
tea-room melodies.

The Twilight of the Birds

I.   *The Lodge, Sandy*

The birds' Valhalla, where at dusk they will come
for the last time and chorus to the earth,
to the fields that are by now shaved clean

of hedgerow, seedpod, stubble, snail.
They will not trouble to debate the issues
passerines have discussed since Chaucer's day –

there is just one way to go: a pilgrimage
to the shores of extinction. The woodpecker
taps their doom in his hanging-cap

and the owl pronounces a verdict on whom-
soever it consumes. The birch-leaves burn
out of the sand, and the only sound

is that dry crackle on the night air.

II.   *Garden Début*

My maiden aunt sat
dying in the living room
and cried out – *Look!*

*Look! there's a woodcock
on the lawn.* And there,
its long beak drawn

before her, he stood
like Siegfried holding out
Nothung, come to release

the Valkyrie as the woodbird
advised. But it was
she who sang out loud

from bronchitic lungs
with all her dicky heart
her immolation scene –

my maiden aunt, who
had seen a woodcock
rode into the night.

III. Interlude

As the swifts play their youthful variations
and fugue about our unlined brows, the young
person's guide to the intricate passions
of the air, we sit outside the Maltings

drinking silence, sublimating the worm:
and *Peter – Peter – Peter!* they all swear
to one who carries his boom out of the storm
far off – a bittern, faint, irregular.

IV. Gaudeamus Igitur

What was that we heard
trapped behind the firescreen
in the staff common room?
No singing, just a desperate
thrashing of wings, as if
the ghost of one of that flock
of black-gowned, beaked
sadistic masters had dropped
back to inspect his ingle,

beating the ignorant soot.
Was it the same stunned
bundle I found by my study
having collided with that ring
of invisible fire, my vitrified
desire not ever to teach?

V.   Heimdall

I am the halcyon at the bridge.
My blue key flashes.
My hologram wings unclick

the barrier, release you to
the bow my speed inhabits.
Kingfisher, heir of the air.

VI.   OM

Ear to the ground
you listen for a melody

and pull out
the serial worm

or crack open
a home key

then, blackbird, in your
old-fashioned evening suit

you will flute
on the top of an elder tree

to the canyons of the stars

100

VII. Of Paradise

An oriole on the islands of the First Cataract.
An osprey in the Nile as I cross on a felucca.
The egrets, white shadows of the sacred ibis.
The hoopoes, exotic moths of the midday flame.

And on the West Bank where the dead make nests
and the Nubians have been made to live in dovecotes,
a bird-catcher from one of the Nobles' Tombs
crouches with his long net, to dam the skies.

VIII. Dodo

Another feather in your cap, my father would say
if I had completed some aberrant course of study
or achieved some groundless acclaim. Flight, flight

is all I want – and if I end up looking like
a Brazilian Indian in my head-dress, still I will not
rise any higher than the cap that fits permits.

IX. Cage-bird

You could not bear it when your mother
let out her budgerigar
to fly about the room, whether

because of some irrational fear
that it would choose to en-
tangle its little claws in your hair

or did it seem to represent
the very madness that was stirring
in your mother's black Victorian

interior, with its whirring
unpredictable wingbeat
and its habit of ignoring

words you had just tried to repeat
(*Hallo. Pretty Boy. Nightnight.*)
and choosing the most unlikely spot

on which to perch, fixing an eye
on you, which says *I'll be going
home soon*, then refusing to fly

back into the cage you are opening?

X. *Tring*

for Michael Walters

At Tring, you guarded a treasury
of the world's eggs, and showed me
that hoard – more precious than Fabergé's
or Fafner's – each egg
a world seen from the apogee
of your craft, keeping its own
atmosphere and global features,
its fabulous lineage, which I
can't now recall, only drawers
like an instrument panel, and rows
of gridlocked shells, the life
blown out of them, their skin-deep
fascination, fragile as eyes.

When the skies above Hertfordshire
are merely home to the Boeing
and the common fighter bomber, these
will still soundlessly glide

open to lay before us
like a lost secret of air
traffic control, your wards:
their speckles, streaks and scrawls.

XI.   Night Calls

Our local doctor
tells of his horror
of owls

of how they will gaze
surgically into your
soft tissue

from the far side of
their barred habitat
their spell of solitary

or wing into your beams
on the way to a
head-on crash

they hoot like doom's
emergency service
and they stand

rubber-necking in the fog
when motorway
madness strikes

their shrieks are the new-
born dead
taking to the darkness

XII. *The Golden Treasury*

They fly up *(clink)* out of the shadow, spark
from forges in the river-bank, or stoop
through frost-giant blue. But my binoculars
just make a double image, I can't hope
to put a name to them. So, then, let's stop
this labelling of what is simply there
and splendidly anonymous! I hear

old Picus mock me hollow, his intruder
alarm's green warning laugh. It taps out Morse
my father would have known how to decode
in airforce grey ... Yes, there is something worse
than extinction, which is namelessness,
and someone has to classify, though time
still holds the net, and nesting is a crime:

to give the oriole its helm and shield,
to ring the eagle, if we must – ensure
our gods can't quite wipe out the lyric world's
Aquila stocks, that there is still the pure
delight of goldfinch on a thistle tower
resisting barbs and traps, building its home
at the bowed twig's end, thrilling to its doom.

Holst

Marching into prayers at primary school
they used to play a 78 of *Mars*.
There began my love of music
and of astronomy. The perfect fool
had found his round peg's round hole:
to sing squarely of the stars
to a generation who would lose its
sight and hearing before it had grown old.

Quartet for a Row
of Terraced Cottages

First violin begins the theme: plainsong
in apple white, a bloom of the sixties, neither
pretty nor bland, yet eastern flavoured, heat
in clay bricks. It hides a small, greenish spark
which keeps on growing, knowing always that once
there grew a sycamore above its sound-box.

Second mirrors the row: a centrifugal
force opens the shared manoeuvring
towards outer space. A touch of a jig
from Ireland, some Italianate trills
and ornamentation, the smiled acceptance
of any wild dissonance from the first.

Viola keeps at arm's length: the ambitious chug
of a fiddle outgrowing its natural size,
self-consciously dull, gawky, wants to be
a bass-line, an oak-beamed original,
but cannot shake the restless mobile grind
of hurdy-gurdy tunes, that gay vulgarity.

Cello knows the long rest is coming, and draws
from its simple well the deepest, oldest tears.
Destined to be low, never to rise or move,
but enjoying others' fireworks, it inhabits
the four autumnal rooms of its clef, desires
no solo, dreaming of song, sweet cadences.

Death in Aldeburgh

The old friends are assembled in the Red House,
are asked to come and voice a brief farewell,
to pitch him their unbroken pure *laudamus*:
the one whom he blazed out, though she was ill
with nerve disease, the one he brusquely sacked
for questioning the joint imperious will,
the one who had not shown sufficient tact
in telling jokes, the one who stood and eavesdropped
on his practising. All those friendships wrecked
the ebb reveals to him, like small roles grouped
for one of his finales, but not singing,
just smiling, thinking, 'Ben, they never stopped
us loving you, those crushing waves and stinging
rebuffs, that icy undertow, each storm,
each murderous calm. We kept on bringing
our scrofulas for your touch to transform –
and you would rise and glow and wave creation's
spring tide across our skins, your light, your warmth
ripening above these manuscript horizons
to light the steep grey shingle of your moods
and stir our mid-life mill-pond with your passions.'

Hepworth

Hers is a headland that invites the awful
gaze, that repels commerce with tanker,
with wrecker, but endures the snatch-sneer

of gulls at an autopsy. She has cut
and polished her buried brightnesses, smoothed
caves out of mind and into flesh.

Fire declares to the bulky stalker
and his flag of convenience: 'My one loyalty
is beyond your horizons!' A school of purposes,

a hump-backed style, are her only rivals –
and whatever secret is reclining where moor
wrests landscape Tregeagle-like to its

desired shape, where holiday spirits
turn to shadows in the underground. To weight.
Taut strings. Tectonic will.

The earth shifting as she tours her own
dark excavation and finds no tin
knocker, but radon: the slow-curing

of her femininity, the sudden combustion of her name,
these blitz the mind this driest of dry
seasons, when no-one thinks of art

and only the sun is a singing perfectionist
keeping an eye on its western gallery
of stones, priceless, permanent, untitled.

At Port Gaverne

The edge draws nearer to the path each day.
Her soft lips open, but in place of speech
a gull cries for its nest and flies away.

A man sees safe ground fall, and starts to pray
he'll make that point he always dreamt he'd reach
(the edge draws nearer to the path each day)

and warn his children in their far-off bay,
miniaturised like counters on the beach:
'A gull cries for its nest and flies away

to some secure and inland home on clay,
but uprooted skies are breaking in that screech!'
The edge draws nearer to the path each day –

whatever warning signs and guidebooks say,
experience alone has power to teach:
a gull cries for its nest and flies away

from plans laid waste. And though a couple stay,
what concrete sea defence can she not breach?
The edge draws nearer to the path each day.
A gull cries for its nest and flies away.

The Source

for Alan Bolesworth

Herodotus was the first to tackle seriously the question of the Nile's source, but he (like the poet) ventured little further south than Aswan. Richard Burton is usually considered the most extraordinary and original of the later explorers, so scandalously attentive was he to every detail of 'primitive' life. Although Burton was undoubtedly the more interesting man, it was Speke who made the most significant discovery of Lake Victoria while under his colleague's 'command', leading to a bitter dispute between them. While Speke was merely tough and a crack shot (besides being very confused about his sexuality), Burton was a superb linguist, prolific writer, translator of The Arabian Nights *and the* Kama Sutra. *His wife, Isabel, was psychically susceptible (a gipsy of the Burton tribe foretold that she would marry a Burton), but also a devout Catholic who never managed to convert her husband and seldom accompanied him on his expeditions. By contrast, Florence Baker – a Hungarian rescued by the genial Sam from a white slave auction – plunged into the direst regions of Africa with her husband. That the two of them survived the 'Sudd' at all is remarkable: that they got through it carrying the contents of a Victorian drawing room is barely credible. Snay bin Amir, who appears at the end of the cycle, was just one of many Arab slave traders who had a stranglehold on Africa at this time.*

Much of the detail in this sequence is to be found in Alan Moorehead's classic The White Nile, *but I am also indebted to Fawn M. Brodie's biography of Burton,* The Devil Drives *and Richard Hall's account of the Bakers,* Lovers on the Nile.

I.   The Source

(Herodotus, 460 B.C.)

The First Cataract, the last
gasp of my journey
out of civilisation, down

a narrowing beam
an intensification of dark
to where there is only

desert and an arrow's
reach of lapis.
In Aswan, I discover

the Source is not to be found
between these pink
granite haunches, where

lotus and crocodile
smile open and the deep-
sunned inhabitants deliver

sparks of blackness
from the annual inundation
singing, singing

that there are two
fountains in the Heart
that the White Man

is looking for and
that the River Nile
will make him blind.

II.   Richard Burton

I have both measured the parts of a Negro in Somaliland
and the sacred black meteorite of Mecca, concealing
the tape in my pilgrim costume like a worm. Recording Angel,
driven by the Arch-Discoverer, through dark I observe
polygamy, infibulation, cannibalism, tastes in fetishes,
castrato-makers, abuse among vice-consuls, effects
of sodomy upon the India List – and I have lost
my reputation, have been upwardly flayed from my footnotes,
seen public insults printed on my own tanned skin.
Disguise. Observation. Classification. And to penetrate
the Holy of Holies.
                    The Nile unwinds like a length
of cortex, swollen with life, quicksilver, rich silt.
The Source is somewhere in that butcher's black from which
comes hurling a javelin that pierces one cheek after the other,
is somewhere in these slow, narcotic thousand-and-one leaves
that I am attempting to translate as she enters frowning, kissing
this scar, this scar ...
                    I can mesmerise any woman
at a hundred miles distance: sheer will
brought her to me, as it has brought me to the peak
of Mount Victoria. Unclean. Satanic. Bestial.

The ritual execution dance of the English journalist –
to communicate his message to posterity, intoxicate the victim,
flatter him, honour him, then strike off his head and drink
a toast to him from the skull. You will not abolish
such a long-sanctioned custom. Oh, I have committed
every sin in the decalogue and am proud of it,
of my skills in thirty languages, of my deadly prowess
as swordsman, scientist, explorer, speaker and writer
of the thousand thousand words that empty the interior
upon the civilised world, this fountain, this inky lake

where nothing is heard of my mother, my father,
not even my wife ...

That is the hyacinth swamp Sam Baker lost his way in.
For me, I will persist in my translation of *The Scented Garden*
and Isabel in her Grand Inquisition. 'Tomorrow,' I tell her,
'I shall have finished this, and then – to our autobiography!'

But I know too that tomorrow Lady Burton will close my eyes
and burn everything.

III.   John Speke

(died of gunshot wounds while hunting in Wiltshire, 1864)

Have asked Petherick to come for a few days
that we may make arrangements for ripping open
Africa together. Too much silence. A capon
keeps following me. England is a haze
beyond the end of these twin barrels raised
towards the Mountains of the Moon and Lord Ripon
holding the Blue ... Load every last weapon!
Roll those women out! What was that useful phrase
Dick tried to teach me? (I have said we'll have
the embryo of a pregnant Kudu doe
when Petherick comes.) Something about satiety
in marriage. Dick Burton could never love
any morsel but his own brains. I used to show
my journals, let him cut things out for me ...

* * *

... At Neston Park, talk to myself, hunt birds.
In Bath tomorrow, cleanse my reputation
of mud, silt, slime. A public confrontation.

113

The Nile is settled. But Burton's skill with words
is swordsmanship. A river flowing outwards
from a lake. I always needed his translation
before I could – but not for that exultation
when alone Speke found the Falls ... Eye on herds
of – what are they? – men, with notebooks, pens
advancing on a stinking water-hole to wallow.
My breech-loader's heavy, has no safety-catch.
I climb towards a stone wall. Sole defence –
Ask him about Karachi – watch him fall
off his perch! Here's my bird. Pretty boy! Touch –

IV. Isabel Burton

For all his languages,

the horoscope of a gipsy
of the tribe of Burton

the dreamscape of a traveller
in a cave in Palestine

the cries of a dumb ape
You terrify me! What is it you want?

defeated him. And this –
the tongues that are his soul

translated into glory,
ashes of his life's magnum opus,

the master twisting the tail
of the beast –

is all for the best.

114

V. *Samuel Baker*

no history   no solid ground   each island
strong enough for a dinosaur to stand on
breaks away to form another colony   the sudd

spawns growth that has no destination   all
shapelessly rotting drift   a preyground
for crocodile and hippopotamus   for mosquitoes

and a hundred jotting flies   birds watch
then laugh us off   the islands shift like a game
of sliding each design into the vacant slot

no man has ever lived here   no woman
wanted children here   the empire of decay
it is an area as large as England

if you find the great lake   what then   what
will you do with it   they ask   the rain
sets in   call it Albert   demands for presents

more beads cups carpets   a better rifle
my fifty guinea gold chronometer
the months tick by   and we cannot move

they offer me a virgin in exchange for my wife
when we try to move   we sink   I watch
Florence fall into a purple clench of corruption

the sun beats us half mad   only the honey
memory   and the what might be   I dream
of the Source   of drinking at the Source

VI. *Florence Baker*

Home is the aim
yet we can make a home
even where no man
no woman
ever dreamt to live.

I was a slave
in Hungary, cannot love
a land throttled by
slavery
as rocks throttle Nile's

power to these Falls –
free, yet it pulls
us down, we plant
vegetables,
adopt pet animals,

losing our will
power, grown stale,
must uproot and shoot
the Falls,
find something to find.

Let us be chained
to nothing, women, men,
except the correct
direction,
that civilising progress.

VII. Snay bin Amir

Two goats, two bullocks
to be sacrificed
in your honour, my friends –

it is not often that we meet
such men of quality
although I am always searching

in my trade, which takes me
on long journeys also,
to Zanzibar, for example,

for the cloves, ah the scent
of cloves! You need me
to protect you from

those little red-hot ant
jaws, the marching columns
that would eat your beds

from under you. My courtyard,
my pure mud vaulting,
my fountain, and a plot

for sugar-cane. Drink tea
and let me teach you words
from three African dialects,

the necessary imperatives,
try them on this girl
who brings the goat meat,

feel her breasts, note
how neatly she is stitched.
Quality, my friends. Eat, eat.

117

The Temple of Horus
a triptych

I

Grand mirror canal –
lead me out of this
black granite shrine

where I am becalmed in
a slave ship, eclipsed
in a solar boat. Take me

from reliefs, posturing
officials, dignitaries
with their clique language

and inflexible stance,
men with heads of beasts
that know only darkness ...

The sun invites. It is
a cat's long stretched
back that leads my touch

by electricity
of night vision
down its eighth life

through hypostyle hall
to vestibule
to court

where the hawk, turning
a blind eye, believes in
himself, and is unruffled.

II

'You will not topple me.
My intelligence
is beyond you, the sweep

of my tail is the curve
of dynasties, and still
I have not had cause

to unfold these wings.
Time enough for that.
I am weighing up

the possibility. Pray
for those who are dust.
Sety's last smile

under glass. Memnon's
silence on the plain.
Pray for spirits

fooled by painted doors
and lapis lazuli
adornments. Pray

for all those who are
nothing but shapes
etched on granite.

They are in my thoughts.
Like my claws in this,
itching for prey.'

III

Vague fallings away to
a strict bottom line.
Vagueness. Another line – like

the horizontal key-shifts
on the djed – the god
Osiris' magic

symbol of lost backbone
enacting its progression
from life to life and after.

This is the Mountain
of the West. This is
the Royal Necropolis.

That figure could be
you, passing through
towards the desert

of a future undreamt
in this rich past
and which has now

arrived in flash-floods.
Watery-eyed, you join
the clouds of babbling dust

to gaze into the blackness.
The guardian with the mirror
guides you back down.